Color by
Lark Pien

SCHOLASTIC INC.

Thanks to Calista Brill, Rachel Stark, and Andrew Arnold at First Second for whipping this book into editorial and production shape, Lark Pien for taking on the ridiculous task of coloring a book in three months and doing it with grace and gusto, Judy Hansen for being my career champion, and Jake Mumm for all the homemade dinners, scooping of cat litter, and general advice and support during a whirlwind creation.

ISBN 978-1-338-61159-5

12 11 10 9 8 7 6 5 4 3 2 1   19 20 21 22 23 24

Printed in the U.S.A.   40

First Scholastic printing, November 2019

Edited by Calista Brill and Rachel Stark
Book design by Chris Dickey
Color by Lark Pien
Song lyrics on pages 37, 39, 77, 109-111, 210-213 by Hellen Jo
Penciled with mechanical #2 pencil, inked with Uni Jetstream ballpoint pen, and colored digitally in Photoshop

For Mama, Baba,
Lynn, and Dr. Smith

CHAPTER ONE

There are only two photos of me.

Oh, I took a bunch but you were mostly in the same pose so I deleted them.

7

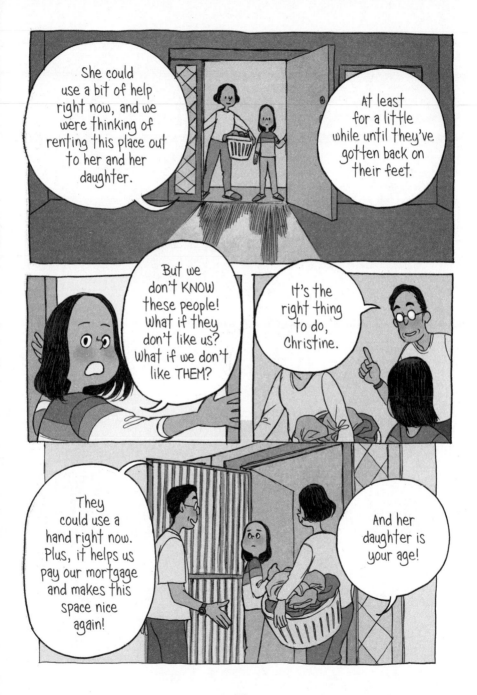

17

CHAPTER TWO

22

Here you go! This is the good fluffy kind with the bears on it. I picked it out myself.

Oh.

Thank you.

Stir
stir

Yeah!

Yeah, girl!

You're doing it! YES!

Feeling that music, keep going!

43

45

舉頭望
明月,

低頭

思故鄉...

床前
明月
光...

CHAPTER FOUR

"누나" 말고 "왕비마마"

I ALSO ANSWER TO CHARA-SAMA

예쁜 공주로 잘못 봤니?

THAT'S NOT MY DESIRE

THIS GIRL TOO FIRE

Nice! So how was your field trip to the observatory today?

It was cool. I tried to find our house through the view-o-scope but I think we're too far.

Mr. Pennypacker bought some astronaut ice cream and we got to try some. It wasn't bad.

Ew. I didn't like it. It was weird.

It's like eating a cookie!

SHOVE

101

床前明月光

疑是地上霜

Moonlight before my bed

Perhaps frost on
the ground.

舉頭望明月

Lift my head and see the moon

低頭思故鄉

Lower my head and
pine for home.

CHAPTER SIX

129

By the way, Christine, I'm really excited for our talent show dance. Can't wait to start rehearsing.

Oh. Yeah, me, too.

I was telling Moon, my mom knows fashion people. She can get us custom jackets.

Maybe Moon can design some outfits for us! Wouldn't that be great?

148

152

CHAPTER SEVEN

The doctors discovered a brain tumor.

Thankfully, we haven't recorded any new seizures since the doctor's visit. But it's lonely for Moon. Maybe Christine could pay her a visit?

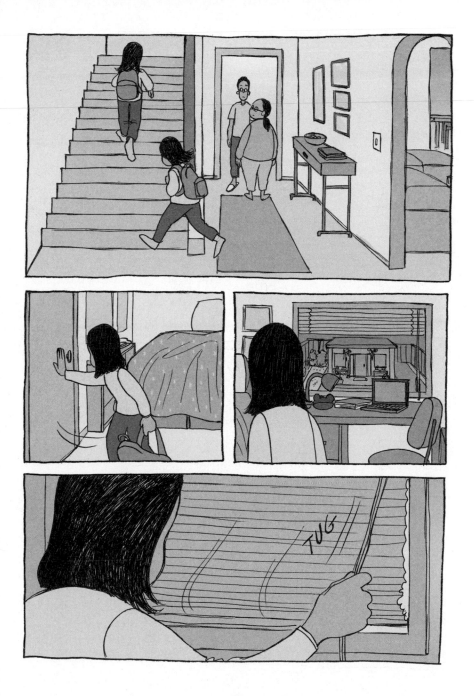

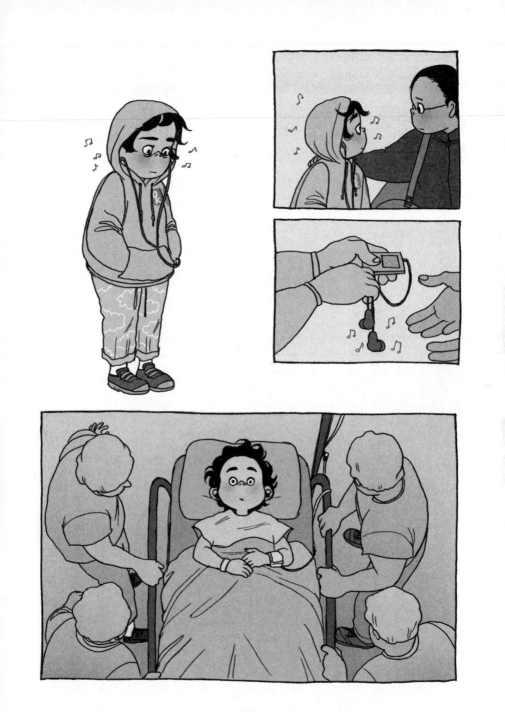

179

SHOVE

Moon's
awake.

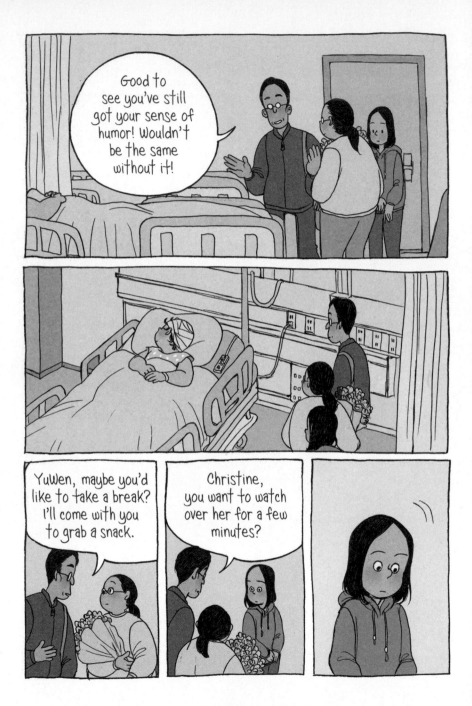

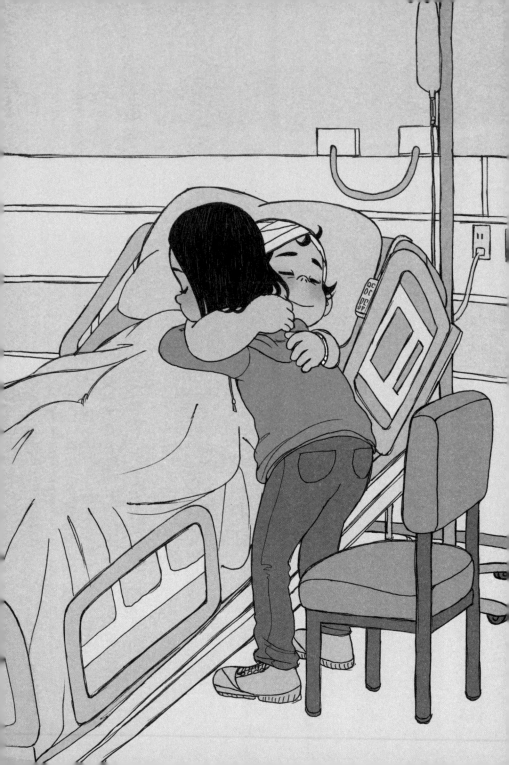

205

Afterword

Stargazing is an entirely fictional story, and yet so much of it is based on real events from my life. When I was six years old, I was diagnosed with a brain tumor just like Moon's. I was too young to realize what was happening, but my vision would go dark and I would see stars and shapes. At first this was fun, and I didn't tell anyone. After all, I thought, wasn't this normal? But eventually the seizures became noticeable, and a few months later I had a surgery to remove the tumor. It was sitting right on top of the visual area of my brain and it came out easily.

The whole ordeal was such a formative part of my childhood that it blends in to everything else. But sometimes I catch myself wondering what my life would be like if things had turned out differently. What if I couldn't read? Or draw? Visual art has become such an important part of my world that it's hard to imagine life without it. I owe so much to my surgeon, Dr. Roderick Smith, the nurses, and my parents for catching the seizures early and making one of the scariest decisions of their life.

Did I see celestial beings during my seizures the way Moon did? No. But I thought they'd be a good way for the book to express how lonely Moon (and I) felt. Like Christine and Moon, I grew up in a region with many other Chinese and Taiwanese immigrant families and their American-born kids. But the more you're expected to share with a group of people, the more you obsess over the ways you are different. (I was vegetarian, I was Buddhist, I didn't excel in academics, I wanted to be an artist, etc.) If I wasn't like the other Asian American kids, who was I supposed to be like?

It's taken me thirty-three years to get to a point where I can comfortably reflect on these feelings. Writing *Stargazing* was as much about healing myself as about showing the diversity of experience even within a very specific community. As our society continues to diversify (as I would hope), I imagine there will be many more Moons and Christines out there wondering which parts of them are "not Asian," and which parts are just uniquely and wonderfully them.

Recovering from the
surgery at the hospital

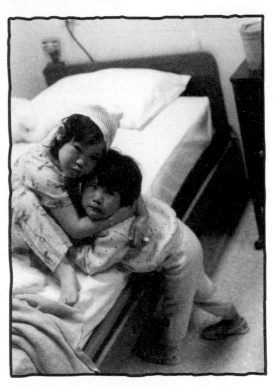

With my little sister,
Lynn, visiting me for
the first time after
the surgery

Jen Wang is the author of *The Prince and the Dressmaker* and *Koko Be Good*, and coauthor of the *New York Times*-bestselling graphic novel *In Real Life* with Cory Doctorow. She is also the cofounder and organizer of the annual festival Comic Arts Los Angeles.

Lark Pien is a cartoonist who also colors. Her color work on *American Born Chinese* by Gene Luen Yang was nominated for an Eisner and won a Harvey award. Other graphic novels she has colored include *Boxers & Saints* (by Gene Luen Yang) and *Sunny Rolls the Dice* (by Matt and Jenni Holm). Her comics have been featured in publications by Fantagraphics, Viz Media, Illustoria, Studygroup, and Random House. She is the author and artist of three picture books, *Long Tail Kitty*, *Long Tail Kitty: Come Out and Play* (with Blue Apple Books), and *Mr. Elephanter* (with Candlewick). She likes to paint with cadmium yellow, antique white, vermillion, burnt umber, and light blue.